After the Walk

The Amazing Places
the Mind Goes

CECILIA ANASTOS

Cecilia Anastos, LLC
P. O. Box 3556
Ramona, CA 92065

ISBN: 978-0-578-28287-9

Cover design by: Tony Serofin
Photo credit: Photo by Shifaaz shamoon on Unsplash

Library of Congress Control Number: 1-11204272491

First Edition: 2022
Printed in the United States of America

Publisher: Cecilia Anastos, LLC - PO Box 3556, Ramona, CA 92065

This book is dedicated to:

My grandmother Magdalena who taught me how to enrich my mind, to my father who passed on to me the gift of dog training, and to all the amazing dogs who have shared these walks with me.

Table of Contents

Preface

First and foremost, thank you for purchasing this book. I appreciate your sense of curiosity to discover what transpires after the walks.

Every day, my dogs and I walk about 2.5 to 3.5 miles around beautiful Ramona, CA. While we walk, I practice walking meditation. My concentration is on the sounds the dogs' paws and my feet make as we touch the ground, their breathing and my breathing, the sound the leaves make when the wind caresses them, and the loud voices of some reactive dogs we encounter along the walk.

This is not a book about meditation or dog training. It is a book about philosophy of life and the wandering mind that flourishes after the walks. If you have ever tried to learn how to meditate, I am sure you have heard that thoughts get into your mind, and you are taught to acknowledge the thought and then go back to the breathing. I have been meditating since childhood; thus, my mind is trained to put those thoughts aside. A few days ago, I decided that they belong in a book.

Have you ever found yourself thinking aloud and having a long dialog with your shadow? It is not being crazy. It is the product of an active mind. This book will touch on those meaningful conversations that I have with my shadow as soon as I return from the walks and I allow my mind to pursue the dialog.

In October 2021, Julie Gallant from the Ramona Sentinel interviewed me, and we talked about my choosing the canvas to express complex feelings. A few months later, I decided to choose the pen to express things for which the canvas would not have been the right medium.

At the time of this writing, my loyal walking buddies were my service dog Nena, her daughters Juliette and Panda, Jolie, Kapa'a, Indie and Luna.

Ramona, California
2022

The Beachcombers

I grew up by the sea. Since early age, I have been an avid walker. My first memories of memorable walks are from the age of 12. My brother and I would walk along the beach from one end to the other.

By the time I was 16 years old, we graduated to hours and hours of walks along the Atlantic coast. We would start at 9 a.m. at a beach called La Perla. We would walk for hours until reaching a lighthouse, and then it was time to turn around.

Now, when I close my eyes, I can still see the sunny days, and the crowds along the beach. My ears hear the sound of the waves make as they reach the end, before turning back. We were always walking on that fine line where the ocean caresses the sand and cools down the feet.

We were walking close to each other, side by side, having the conversations of the century, singing our favorite songs from Pink Floyd, Yes, Rush, Sui Generis, and Joan Manuel Serrat. Avid readers since childhood, there was always a topic that would make our imaginations run unleashed, and create a world where everything was working like a Swiss watch.

My brother always walked on my left side. It was then I decided to wear my watch on my right hand to prevent it from bumping on my brother's right hand. I have maintained that fashion. I still wear my watch on the right hand. When I close my eyes, I continue to imagine a world where things really always work nicely —like a Swiss watch.

During those walks, we talked about the tribulations of life that captured the mind of two adolescents growing up in an upper-middle-class Italian family. We knew we were destined to leave that town. We planned our professional lives. We dreamed about adventures we wanted to embark on. My brother and I were since he was born like butt and underwear, always together.

One day, we stopped by the yacht club to visit with Atilio. Atilio worked at the club. He was always helping my parents with their sailboat, and for us he was an adopted uncle. As we approached the marina, we saw a sailboat with a French flag. At the time, my brother was fluent in French and I was not yet.

We decided to approach the sailboat to inquire whether they were sailing around the world and to offer our help in any way we could. This is how we met Eric Valli, who is now a famous photographer for National Geographic and lives in Nepal, his girlfriend at the time, Christine de Cherisier, and the other couple were Phillip and Sarah (I cannot remember their last names). We switched to English so I could join the conversation as well. This was the encounter that set my brother and me to the planning of sailing around the world.

After the Walk

Mar del Plata

We spent a full month with Eric and his crew. We took them to town to buy spare parts for the sailboat, acted as translators, showed them the best places to eat fresh fish — the places only the locals know.

It was the end of the summer when Eric and his crew had to continue their journey and my brother and I had to go back to school. We stayed in touch with Eric for many years. Then, he stopped writing when he moved to Nepal.

Off till the next walk!

Longevity

It is my ultimate goal to live until I am 122 years old. The exact number of years come from the lifespan of French citizen Jeanne Louise Calment who died at the age of 122 years and 164 days.

Longevity is something that became a goal for me when I turned 18. I went to live on my own and I had total control of my diet. My grandparents lived a long life. My American paternal grandfather lived till the age of 98, his wife lived till 94, and my Spaniard maternal grandfather lived till 90. My Italian maternal grandmother, unfortunately, died at the age of 65. She had liver cancer.

Needless to say, none of them were mindful about their diets. My grandpa smoked cigars. My grandma practically lived on beef alone. She thought only rabbits eat vegetables. In spite of their choices of food and lifestyle, they all had the common denominators for longevity that Daniel Buettner identified in his book The Blue Zones — a network of friends, daily walks, a glass of wine, nuts, a passion for books, and a family that loved them till the end of the world.

My grandma Magdalena played tennis and every year till the year she passed away, she met with all her colleagues for a lunch reunion. She invited me to one of them and I was so moved and fascinated by the conversations of these octogenarians and nonagenarians.

That same year, at the yacht club where I grew up sailing, I met a lady in her 80s who looked like she was in her 50s. It was the deciding point for me that I wanted to do whatever it would take to live a long and healthy life.

Did I have a perfect diet all the time? Nope. I had my share of cakes and chocolate. Alcohol was not part of my equation; however, I would get "drunk" on chocolate and masas finas and masas secas (an exquisite delicacy from Belgium, France, Switzerland and Argentina).

In the 90s, I embraced full throttle the Paleolithic diet. I realized that sugar was increasing the frequency of my panic attacks. I made a comment about that to Suzanne G. who was managing one of the polo teams at the Del Mar Polo Club. She introduced me to the famous paleo diet. I spent that decade reading everything of value on the topic of extending life beyond the average. My Miracle Brain and The Okinawa Program are the two books that most influenced my diet from that point forward.

By the turn of the XXI century, I noticed the topic of longevity became the ultimate goal of many. In fact, in 2015, Megan Friedman writing for Esquire Magazine published an article about two longevity experts, Dmitry Kaminskiy and Dr. Alex Zhavoronkov, who placed a $1 million bet on who lives past the age of 100. The terms of the bet state that whoever dies first, after passing the age of 100, pays the $1m.

Because of the many variables involved in longevity, I have to focus on the things that are under my control such as diet and lifestyle. I am aware of all the other variables that could cut my life short without my having causing it – accidents, natural disasters, being the victim of a violent crime, wars, and pandemics. As I write these lines, we are entering the second Winter with the COVID-19 virus flying among us, and the book The Blue Zones by Dan Buettner is now becoming quite popular.

I remember the conversation I had, a while ago, with my friend Wolf A. I was taking my vitamins and measuring food, and he asked whether the stress of following an eating plan so closely was counter-productive to the goal of longevity. It was a great question that kept me thinking for a long time. I must say that I have to agree with him. He made me realize that this extreme focus on what I put or not put inside my body is similar to thinking very hard about not thinking during meditation. I managed to reach a balance where I am mindful about my eating plans; however, I do not stress out about the desire of longevity.

As I write this book, my diet is based on fish as the only source of animal protein, fruits, walnuts and an array of leafy vegetables; as well as French, pinto and garbanzo beans. I walk between 2.5 to 5.5 miles a day. I sleep 8 hours at night, and take my traditional nap after work. My Italian ancestors were adamant about these naps, and I am not planning on interrupting that tradition.

After the Walk

I often ponder on the following questions – is our lifespan determined at birth? Is our lifespan influenced by astrological factors – meaning the time of our birth?

As a Zen Buddhist, I believe in reincarnation. Is our destiny affected by the past lives we carry within our aura?

Off till the next walk!

Walk and Talk

Every year, my mother would spend several weeks with me at the ranch in Virginia. The house was in a cul-de-sac and it was about a mile long between the house and the end of the cul-de-sac. This is the countryside and houses are spread apart and beautiful green lawns surrounds them in the Spring and Summer months.

My mom and I loved to walk. Every afternoon after work we took my son who at the time of this story was about 9 years old, and the dogs for a walk. We walked along the road to the end of the cul-de-sac and back. On some occasions, if I had not had the time to exercise my horse Dakota, he would walk by our side with halter on as if he were another dog.

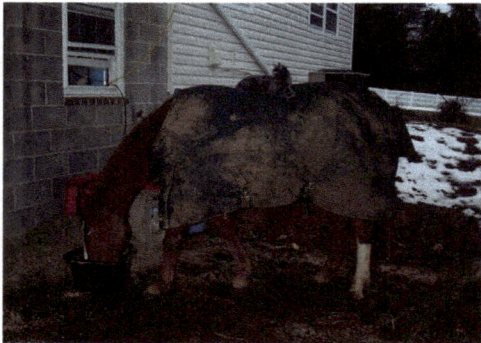

Dakota with cat Grigio on top

One day, my son was not in the mood to walk at all. I did not want to leave him alone in the house. I convinced him that walking was good for his health, and it was good for grandma and me. Finally, with the typical rebellious attitude that a 9-year old could display, he joined the walk.

On that particular day, he was very chatty with me. He and I talked all the way up to the end of the cul-de-sac. My son was talking in a whiney voice and at full speed, and at times almost whispering to me. Although my mother spoke English fairly well, it was difficult for her to hear him and follow the conversation.

When we turned around to return home, my son became silent. It gave my mother the opportunity to start talking with me. I must say that she was also a chat box so I am pretty sure she had to use extra control to keep herself from interrupting the conversation my son and I had been having.

When it was my mom's turn to talk, she told me she was so happy that my son and I had such a fluid communication. She was so happy about how much he was talking with me, and she started going on and on about how important it is to have dialog with our children. Finally, I could not resist anymore and I started laughing my brains off. She looked at me with consternation until I managed to explain to her why I was laughing so loudly.

During the entire dialog my son and I had, the conversation was nothing other than him asking "why do we need to walk?; I am tired of walking, can we go back? How many more minutes are we going to walk? I do not like walking, why do I have to come along? Why can't you and Nelci walk without me? How far is the cul-de-sac?" I was politely replying to each question with the appropriate answer that, to my mother's ears, it sounded as if we were having the most meaningful conversation a mother and son could have.

Off till the next walk!

Sunday Meetings at the Park

Every Sunday morning, a group of alcoholics anonymous individuals meet under the roofed patio of Collier Park. This particular Sunday, as I was entering the park, I noticed a much larger crowd than usual. Ramona, in California, is a small town of only 20,000 dwellers and it caught my attention how many people seem to have problems with alcohol addiction.

I do not drink alcohol for philosophical reasons. In spite of the rationalization that has been spread about one glass of wine a day to thin the blood and prevent clots, I believe alcohol has no benefits to our health. You can drink 8oz of organic grape juice and get the same amazing nutrients of the grapes without the alcohol.

I believe alcohol destroys lives. The drunk driver who kills an innocent bystander leaves behind a devastated family. The drunk driver that dies leaves a devastated family. The drunk spouse that takes it out on the children and the spouse leaving bruises and broken bones; as well as wounds on the soul that never heal.

My father was a functional alcoholic, i.e., the type that does not drink during working hours, however, this person cannot stop watching the clock for that moment of the evening when, according to society norms, it is normal to start drinking. For him, the justification to drink a full bottle of wine on his own was associated with dinner time.

I call those individuals dry alcoholics. During the day, they have the bad temperament and short fuse from the lack of ethanol in their systems. Then, as the first drink reaches their system and, for a short period of time, you see a pleasant personality flourishing. This is short lived because when the last drop of the bottle is drunk, the aggressive personality flourishes in some of these individuals. Others passed out and the next day cannot recall a single sentence of the conversation they were having with themselves or whoever had to endure that nonsense tirade of thoughts.

With my father, I could not tell whether the alcohol was making him aggressive or the fact that he could not drink a second bottle during dinner time because my mother would object, or society in general would object, or he would be forced to label himself as an alcoholic if he dared to drink a second bottle.

I was fortunate enough that he never addressed his ire on me. Neither with his fists or his words. Nevertheless, his actions toward my mother left me with scars on my nervous system to the point that it contributed to my developing panic attacks. He was verbally abusive. He would scream at her for a long hour every single night. He only landed a hand on her once. I was old enough to warn him that if he ever raised his hand against her again, he was going to deal with my wrath. After all, it was his idea for me to learn Krav Maga. Can you imagine having to walk on egg shells every single evening of your life, every single weekend and holiday for fear that whatever you did could set his ire off?

We never knew what it was going to set the ire off. One day, my parents and I were having dinner with my boyfriend at one of my favorite restaurants in Carmel Valley, CA. My mother had ordered a salad with the crunchy croutons. She was eating it like anybody else, and all of sudden the monster inside my father overtook the dinner. He screamed at her for chewing too loudly, and he banged his fist on the table. It was the first day they were meeting my boyfriend —the man who eventually became my husband and the father of my child.

We now know that alcoholism is a disease. As with other diseases, it means that alcoholic individuals have a genetic marker that makes them prone to chemical dependencies. The advances in the field of genetics are amazing. We should jump on these advances and get a DNA profile on all young adults after they turn 18 years of age. Wouldn't it be wonderful to know that one has to be away from alcohol for life because the likelihood of turning into an alcoholic is super high?

Ironically, I like to paint still life and figurative paintings of wine and champagne bottles. The beauty of the wine glass reflecting natural light captivates me. I ponder on the mystery of the ethanol and grapes contained in that bottle. Grapes and ethanol together have held some magic power for centuries —they have had so many individuals hooked on them.

When I paint, I do not think of the damage my alcoholic father caused to my soul. When I am in front of the canvas, I focus on the beauty of the palette I have chosen for my paintings. The sarcastic humor behind them, such as my paintings of the bottles with the name of the Untouchables who brought down Al Capone during the Prohibition Era.

Wine and Fruit (2021)

To those who are attending AA meetings and stay off alcohol for good, I take my hat off to you and congratulate you. For those who cannot seem to find a way to keep the bottle away, I send you my Bodhisattva strength to aid you in finding a higher purpose and accomplishing the ultimate goal of never drinking alcohol again.

Off till the next walk!

Dreams Interrupted

A few stories ago, I told you about my plans to sail solo around the world. My brother and I had a giant world map poster in our room, and after that magic summer when we met Eric Valli, we began reading books about other yachtsmen and yachtswomen who have sailed in solitary around the world. On that map, we marked the port towns where we were planning to stop.

We made lists on how to prepare the food needed, the best routes to take, the best type of sailboat, and on and on. Together, we spent three years planning our sailing around the world in solitary.

In March 1981, I was leaving the University after class and suddenly I could not walk any further. I felt that everything was spinning and I lost perception of depth. I could not tell whether the curb was 6 inches high or 6 feet high. I grabbed the column of the street light. A friend helped me reach my dorm. Frantically, I called my parents who at the time were living 90 minutes away from my dorm.

My father was a Ph.D. in Analytical Chemistry with a vast knowledge of medicine. He suspected a neurological illness, and he was concerned that he was too far away, and I needed to be seen right away. Thus, my parents called their best friend, Dr. Roberto Viola, who came over right away and did a thorough neurological exam. He told my parents the diagnostic was inconclusive. He could not find any physiological impairment. It was not until 1991 that I learned the name of this terrifying thing that was taking control of my body.

For the next 7 years after the first dizzy spell, I continued life as usual minus the interruptions that the severe anxiety I was developing was causing to my body. Anxiety is like a tick that likes to latch onto the skin. My anxiety liked to latch onto the lining of my stomach so I developed a painful gastritis. Even though I was living life in full, there was always that shadow of pondering when the next dizzy spell was going to show up unexpectedly and with a whim of its own.

The dreams of sailing in solitary around the world were finally interrupted for good when I got the second full-blown and paralyzing dizzy spell. I had just finished my final exams, and I was returning home in a bus. Suddenly, I felt the whole bus was going upside down, my hands were folding inwards and my legs were no longer moving at my will. The lady next to me realized that something was seriously wrong. She asked where I lived. We were not far from the apartment I shared with my brother. She asked the bus driver to please stop the bus right in front of the apartment where I was living with my brother.

She rung the bell, my brother rushed downstairs and when he saw me, he rushed me in a taxi to the emergency room of the German hospital. My brother was studying biochemistry at the time, and like my father, he was also well-versed in medicine.

The doctor asked many questions about my life style. My brother explained to him that I have treated my body like a temple since I was 18, and that I had just finished the final exams. He then told us that whatever I had suffered was caused by acute stress. He sent us home with a benzodiazepine to take in case of another one of these episodes.

It was frightening for me, my brother and the taxi driver, to whom my brother asked to drive as fast as he could, as if he were an ambulance. I do not remember much about the moment we got into the taxi and we reached the hospital. I do remember that I had laid down on the back seat of the cab with my head on my brother's legs while he was holding my hands which were folding inwards. I was shaking from head to toes. I had lost all perception of depth, as it happened in 1981. I thought I had been accidentally poisoned.

Although I knew at that moment that I could not sail around the world, I was determined to continue my life in full production. I was not going to let this setback screw up all of my plans. However, every big change in lifestyle would bring again those episodes.

The next big waves of attacks happened when I met my ex-husband and we moved in together. The experts say that one of the biggest stressors in life is moving. Bingo.

In the middle of one of those attacks, we ended up in the emergency room of the University of California San Diego Medical Center and we had the absolute fortune of meeting an intern who told us that she had seen patients with similar symptoms, and doctors were calling that phenomena panic attacks.

It took 10 years from the first episode to get a name for that crazy thing that was taking control of my entire body. I learned then that having the name of a syndrome is like grabbing a life ring thrown at you when you are floating in the middle of the ocean. The intern also referred us to a holistic doctor in Chula Vista, Dr. John Pullen, who had designed a special set of mind exercises to keep the panic attacks at bay. He became my miracle doctor, and it is because of him and his program that I was able to give birth to my beautiful child several years later.

Off till the next walk!

The Oligarchy of Medicine

*** The following write-up is my opinion only. This does not constitute a medical advice in any shape or form, nor am I asking you to flush your pills down the toilet. This is my opinion, and my choice of lifestyle. ***

Big pharma and longevity are dichotomies. The moment you begin popping pills produced by big pharma, you can kiss your dreams of longevity good bye. Big pharma is in the business of making sure you continue being ill with one thing or another. How do you think they make the billions of dollars?

For example, if you are constantly taking Ibuprofen for headaches and other pains, you are creating leaky gut. This means that protein and lipocytes molecules escape your gut into the blood stream.[1] This will elevate your triglycerides for which you will be asked to take statins which in turn might cause another array of messes in your body. The list of this kind of pharmaceutical dominos goes on and on.

I am fully aware of some lifesaving medications such as antibiotics and vaccines, and I do take them when appropriate and needed. I am not against all medical advances, or products. I am just puzzled at

---

[1] I did not make this thing up. You can read more here https://www.healthline.com/nutrition/is-leaky-gut-real

the need to take a pill for any discomfort the body might express. Many of these discomforts can be mitigated with a change in dietary and lifestyle habits.

Endobiogenic medicine and other forms of alternative medicine treat the body as a holistic entity. This means that if you have a headache, you will not receive just a pill for the headache. Your entire body and lifestyle will be closely analyzed to discover the cause of the headache.

Unfortunately, insurance companies do not want to cover these types of treatments in spite of the fact that there is plenty of documentation about the beneficial effects to health, the amount of productivity gained by workers because they are spending less time on sick leave, etc., etc.

Naturopathic practitioners and endobiogenic doctors are expensive. A long time ago, I began thinking about the oligarchy of medicine. The charges can go from $90 to $600+ per consultation. Obviously, this is a service for the few who can afford it.

I understand that these individuals need to pay bills and make a living. I find that those who charge more than $200 per visit practice the wrong intention. Right intention is studying medicine or medical related disciplines to assist other sentient beings in living as healthily as they possible can. In trying to become rich in the process of assisting others, these individuals are creating an oligarchy of their profession, and practicing wrong intention.

If these individuals want to enjoy expensive lifestyles, they should have pursued an MBA or chosen other profession that would have afforded them that lifestyle. When it comes to disciplines related to the improvement of the health of sentient beings, then compassion must be seriously considered even when embracing it would lead to a modesty in lifestyle.

Off till the next walk!

Will

Do not get all excited because I am not talking about William here. I am talking about the will, the faculty by which a person decides on and initiates a particular action.

Albert Einstein has been quoted as saying "there is a force more powerful than steam, electricity and atomic energy: willpower."

Are some of us born with it? Do we acquire it in schools or through the guidance of mentors? Why is it that some people cannot seem to get their ass off the couch even when presented with a compass and detailed instructions on how this willpower thing works?

It consumes all of my Buddha patience to see someone with potential who is not willing to put in the minimum effort to move from point A forward to accomplish more in life. By accomplishing more in life, I mean in a way that does not create unnecessary friction on oneself, others, or the environment.

Now, you may start to think about the definition of success; that will be the topic of another walk.

Off till the next walk!

Number 3

I noticed that in the United States when one wants to be polite to refer to bathroom events, society has decided that Number 1 is liquid and Number 2 is the solid.

I also noticed that people here fart without warning and often mask that sound with a cough. The problem is that they cannot mask the horrible odor that often accompanies their flatulencies.

I wonder why nobody calls Number 3 before the incoming disgusting, noxious, putrid, festering odor. A warning will provide the people standing by the fart-dropper the chance to duck and cover their noses.

In golf, the players yell, "Fore!", which is an English homonym of "Four". During World War I, soldiers were yelling "Gas, Gas, Gas!" as they were ringing the bell.

At least in the height of the pandemic, we were somewhat protected when wearing our masks.

Off till the next walk!

White Hair

It has been decided – I am no longer covering my white hair. I used to cover the roots when the first strands of white hair started showing up. My father had a completely white head by the age of 40. I did not fall too far from the apple tree in that department.

I have three auto-immune diseases and I am concerned about putting chemical products on my scalp. The decision has nothing to do with this newly developed fashion of some that surged during the pandemic. It has to do with feeling a rejection at skin level of some chemical products.

Last year, the newspaper The Guardian did an interview with Sofia Loren where she said "The body changes. The mind remains the same." This phrase reminded me that we all have to come to terms with aging; however, aging of the physical appearances does not necessarily imply aging of the soul.

I look at myself in the mirror and I see a woman with no wrinkles, white hair roots of about two inches and a beautiful and unique mind. Inside, I feel 20 years younger than what my age on paper dictates.

My grandma was adamant about the cultivation of the mind in preparation for this moment. She seeded my brain for me to become the intellectual and erudite I am now.

My grandmother and I

It is better to be a wise woman, with or without white hair, than a colored-hair bimbo.

Off till the next walk!

A Word with You

Several times a week, the dogs and I walk for many miles. Elaine, the nurse who works with one of my doctors, told me to walk in a way that I could not have a conversation with a person walking beside me.

The following is a conversation that took place among the dogs during one of those walks when I was feeling ultra-energetic, and I think the pace was even faster than usual. The dogs were Juliette, a 16-month old Golden Retriever, her mother Nena, a 4-year old Golden Retriever, who is also my service dog, and Jolie, a 9-month old German Shepheard Dog.

Juliette: Why are we walking so fast?

Jolie: Because that gal, whatyoumacall her, told her so!

Nena: Her name is Elaine, I was there when she asked Ceci to walk as fast she can. They were talking about how people who walk a lot and fast live to pass 100 years of age. It is Ceci's goal. I am older than you two. If I can keep up, you can keep up.

Juliette: Well, you are her service dog so it is not that you have a choice. I could stay in the kennel and then run all over the yard.

Jolie: I hope the lady I am going to serve does not go for these crazy fast walks.

Juliette: Hello! You are going to live in Maui part of the year, girl. What do you think people do there? They walk along the beach all day long!

Jolie: Tell your mom to signal that Ceci's system is not working well.

Juliette: She will never do anything like that.

Jolie: Then, you do it. You know how it is done.

Juliette: Ceci only listens to my mom. Plus, it is not honorable. Why don't you do it?

Jolie: Of course, I won't! I am a German Shepherd Dog and we have a reputation for accuracy and loyalty.

Juliette: Oh yeah? And why do you think a Golden Retriever will go ahead with your stupid ideas about a false positive?

Nena: Hush the two of you! Arguing about these walks will not change Ceci's pace. You are missing the beauty around you, and the new smells that showed up with yesterday's rain.

Jolie: Next time you and Ceci see Elaine, tell her the rest of the dogs want to have a word with her.

Off till the next walk!!

Free Money

An armored track was traveling North along the I-5 freeway somewhere in Southern California when all of a sudden the back door opened and bags of money started flowing onto the freeway.

All the bills were green color, however, the provenance of the money was unknown. Some of those bills could have been earned legally and under an ethical compass. Others could have been passed around by unscrupulous individuals who make money by making the lives of others miserable, whether it is through slavery, drug addiction or any of the vicious cycles that humanity has been battling for centuries.

The freeway became a parking lot. Cars were not moving. People were chasing the bills while filming themselves doing so. Then, they were having the courage, nerve or stupidity of posting those photos in social media.

I was mesmerized at the spectacle of the stupidity of the masses. I wanted to ask any of them what they were expecting to happen next. Did they think they could walk into an expensive store and start paying with stolen bills whose numbers were already being tracked? For those who posted on social media, I guess they had missed the chapter on how to rob a bank and not tell anybody about it.

I do not believe in free money. I have always worked for mine. When I was pregnant, I attended a conference organized by the Montley Fools – The Gardner Brothers. First thing I learned was "stop playing the lotto and invest those dollars into an account that will yield through compound interest."

Not long ago, I read a book titled The Psychology of Money. First line in the book... Do not play lotto.

Off till the next walk!

Them Chickens

Talking about free and easy money, I remembered an incident that took place while I was living in Virginia.

One day, a young neighbor of 21 years of age came to the house to tell me that I had to pay him $150 because two of my dogs had broken into his chicken coop and killed them chickens.

I was devastated that my Great Dane named Pirate and his best buddy, an Australian Shepherd named Brandy, had done that. I apologized profusely, and asked him how many of "them chickens" were killed. He said two.

Because I did not know what "them chickens" were, and the price seemed quite high at the time, I told this young man that I was going to do some research and help repair the damage.

I went to the Google Search and typed "them chickens" because I wanted to know what kind of chickens these were and the reason they would cost so much money. All I was getting were pictures of regular chickens.

Then, I called my friend Ernie who is well-versed in many things and I was sure he was going to be able to guide me in the right direction.

Brandy and Pirate

First, he started laughing and I let it run because I thought he was laughing at my dogs' troublemaking endeavors. Then, he switched to his educational tone and told me in certain terms – "Ceci, that is the way the people in that area talk. Them chickens, them dogs, them whatever! Your dogs killed two regular chickens that you can get at Tractor Supply for a few bucks."

Of course, I could then not stop laughing. I went to Tractor Supply, bought two of the "them chickens" and fixed the problem with a few bucks.

We both learned a lesson – mine was about language in the area; and for the young man, he learned not to try to pull my leg again.

Off till the next walk!

The Other Half After the Divorce

During the second year of the pandemic, two friends broke the news to me that they were getting a divorce. One with two young children, and the other with no children. They both told me "I would like to have a relationship with my ex- like the one you built with yours."

Before we dive into serious business about divorces, may I suggest some movies that will help you pass the evenings? 1) Something's Gotta Give starring Jack Nicholson, Diane Keaton, Keanu Reeves and other excellent actors; 2) It's Complicated starring the one and only Meryl Streep, Steve Martin, and Alec Baldwin; and 3) The War of the Roses starring Michael Douglas, Kathleen Turner and Danny DeVito.

Regardless of the amount of time you were married, there is a half of you that merged into the other half. The merging takes place without us being aware of it. It is part of the daily compromises we make when we fall in love. We change a little of our routine and the other half changes a little of his or her routine to adjust to yours, and so on.

When the divorce happens and you find yourself without that person, you must become a whole again. It is very important that you take your time to find the half person that was merged with the other half. While you discover again the half that was somehow merged into your ex-spouse and you strive to become a whole, you must make peace with the situation. The reality that your marriage ended. You are on your own. It will take a good six plus months for you to discover who you really are again.

Notice that I have used the word must in the paragraph above. You probably wonder who the fuliculi am I to tell you what you must do. It is because these two things – becoming a whole, and making peace with the fact that you are divorced– are essential if you want to continue having a civilized relationship with your ex-partner.

Maybe you divorced because your partner was cheating on you, or because your husband told you that his male friend was giving him more pleasure, or you might have divorced because the delicate web of romance and sensuality that holds a marriage together was gone and you were living as polite roommates. If you have children, you must think about them first and put aside the anger and desire of revenge you might feel against your partner.

Some divorces last years because one or both sides want more and more, and the anger consumes the lives of the litigious partner, and ruins the lives of the children. I remember the Betty Broderick case.

If you, the reader of this book, is the one who wants to maintain a friendly relationship with your ex-partner, then you are the one who has to learn to pick up the battles that are worth fighting.

Money is not one of them. It is not worthy. Making sure the other side respects the custody schedule for the children, yes, it is a worthy battle to fight.

As a Zen Buddhist, I believe in the power of the mind. We are what we think. If you spend all day thinking about how horrible the person you have just divorced is or was during the marriage, you will attract unwholesome energy and you will not be able to move forward.

In the end, who knows what it is good and what it is bad. Maybe, you discovered that the divorce actually was the best thing that could have happened to you because you flourished in a new career or ended up finding the love of your life, etc.

Everything in life has a beginning and an end. You can imagine this concept as a circle. We cannot always dictate the diameter of the circle – meaning, we cannot always say that my marriage will last 50 years and that circle will have a huge diameter, or that my employment in my current profession will last six months with a small diameter because I have discovered a new profession that is more attractive. Nevertheless, the wise person accepts the end of the circle and does not fight to try to keep something going that has reached its natural end.

When you reach the end of the marriage circle, you can think of the new friendship circle, think of the new friendship circle you can begin with your ex-spouse. Anger, resentment, jealousy, comparing yourself to whoever your ex-partner is now dating are unwholesome emotions that keep you stagnated. Stagnated water grows putrid smells.

Flowing water brings freshness and new leaves and twigs.

Off till the next walk!

Don Agustín y El Gato Bafico-Rojas

When I was just 18 years old, I was hanging out at the yacht club with Don Agustin and El Gato Bafico-Rojas. El Gato was super excited because he had bought his microtoner sailboat that he named Uno. Don Augustin asked him why he had named the sailboat Uno. El Gato said because he was going to be number one in all the regattas.

Don Augustin asked who the skipper was going to be, and El Gato pointed at me and said "Talent and beauty, she is my skipper." I asked El Gato to let me bring a friend of mine named Archi with whom I had sailed for the past two years in his own sailboat named Kenyenkon. El Gato said yes, and Uno's first crew was established.

I had the enormous pleasure of being Uno's first skipper and winning the regatta. It was a Buenos Aires-Riachuelo-Buenos Aires.

Don Agustin and Archi were also crew members of a Frers 44 named Soleil, and I wanted badly to be part of that crew. After winning the first leg of the race, I asked Don Agustin if he would talk to the Soleil's captain (Mataco Tossi) to inquire whether he could bring me as part of the crew. Don Agustin said that I needed to prove my cooking skills that night before he could make up his mind.

Dinner was delicious and two weeks later I was on board of the Soleil. Mataco put only one condition – I had to wear a bikini with prints of the sun. I found the bikini and it became the summer attire while I was on board.

As I was walking the dogs today, a flash of hundreds of memories crossed my mind about my days on board of the Soleil. On the first race we did abroad, we slept overnight. My friends, Archi and Eduardo, wanted to pull a joke on Don Agustin. While we were all asleep, they put Don Agustin's underwear half hanging from my bed, as if he had been there during the night. The funny thing is that he was about 40 years older than me. We all looked at him as if he were our wise grandpa.

The Buenos Aires-Sauce-Buenos Aires Regatta, and the guys telling me the mast needed to be checked out. Because I was the lighter one of the crew, I was going to be hoisted up. Years later, I learned it was a trick so Martin B. could take photos from below.

The afternoon before the Florianopolis Regatta that Archi, Eduardo and I spent securing the bunkbed violins so Mataco could not use any single bunk without going through the painful task of undoing hundreds of knots.

My spending hours trying to get Juan Jose M. fever down while we were in Puerto Sauce; and listening to all the goofy stuff the guys had to say about that.

I was a young girl and a virgin. At night, I would listen to the guys talking about girls. They thought

After the Walk

I was asleep already; however, I had my radar up. Then I would ask my mom "what does it mean this and that?" She would always say "Ceci, where did you hear that!?"

Eduardo had a sign at the entrance of the sailboat's cabin that read "Al ped is reempujaris quand pichilus cortus est." I asked him what it meant. He said it was Latin and that one day I was going to figure it out on my own. I did! Four years later. In English, it could translate as "it is useless to keep pushing when your penis is short."

I spent 4 years sailing on board the Soleil. It was the last sailboat I raced on. It was time again for me to move to another pasture.

Don Augustin sadly has passed away already. As I write this book El Gato is 83 years old, and he still remembers me as "talento y belleza."

Off till the next walk!

Dusty Friday

Every Friday, at the park across from my house, the park keeper passes the machine that evens the dirt. His duties at the park seem to be on a fixed schedule because every week it is the same routine.

Today, the wind is blowing at 45 mph, and the keeper is passing the darn machine.

My mind was wondering about critical thinking. The freedom of making decisions based on the current conditions rather than being an automated two-legged following a routine that no longer makes sense.

Off till the next walk!

Impermanence

Zen Master Thich Nhat Hanh passed away on January 22, 2022, and he reminded me again of the impermanence of all sentient beings. Although he is no longer physically present in this world, he left a very rich legacy with his writings and the many Zen monasteries he founded all over the world.

I am fully aware of the impermanence of sentient beings and as Zen Buddhist, I also believe in reincarnation. As members of society, we have an obligation to contribute in meaningful ways to the betterment of all sentient beings. Some individuals leave books, others music, paintings or other forms of art, and life-changing discoveries in science and technology.

I pick up my iPhone, and I think of Steve Jobs' legacy. I can read Frankl's Man's Search for Meaning over and over again. I play Ravel's Bolero at full volume and I feel his obsession with repetition, which unfortunately was an indication of the beginning of his Alzheimer's disease.

I am also aware of those who left an invaluable legacy on me even though, they did not write a book, or invent anything related to science and technology, or composed a piece of music. It was done by the one-on-one teachings that with patience and love were guiding me toward a life of successes.

I want to recognize some of them here: My paternal grandmother, Magdalena, to whom I owe the woman I am today; Nick Lore to whom I owe one of my professional paths; My aunt Ivonne "Monona" de Pablo who was my absolute model of what a businesswoman with a plan can accomplish, and as she would always tell me… "Ceci, avanti. Sempre avanti[2]"; and my German Shepherd Dog Maximus von der Grafschaft Mark who inspired me to found my canine school Meridus K9 & Equine.

I leave to my son and to others a collection of paintings, a collection of writings, well-trained pets and service dogs, and hours of teachings about Zen Buddhism, stoicism and cyber defense.

What is the legacy you want to leave behind in this world when your body is no longer physically present?

Off till the next walk!

---

[2] Move forward. Always move forward.

Success

Some people define success in direct relationship with the amount of money they earn.

I define success in direct relationship with accomplishing goals at the professional and personal levels. I am also very aware that we control 90% of everything we do. However, there is that tricky 10% where we have no control and it can stop us from being successful in a particular area.

Could I have succeeded as another solo female sailing around the world? Nope. The panic attacks got the upper hand on this one. Did I end up bitter and feeling victimized by my own wacky nervous system? Nope. I moved on happily and looked forward to finding the next goal or challenge that was up to my capabilities.

For those who define success in direct relationship with money, do you have a stopping point? For example, is a million enough or do you want a billion? When I read the book the Psychology of Money by Morgan Housel, I learned about a concept named "enough" which some individuals lack. The author presents some examples of individuals who were rich and wealthy at the time they decided to commit crimes, such as insider trading or monumental ponzi schemes.

The lack of enough can also be applied to any other disciplines where an individual is after success at all cost, however, it seems that the pinnacle of glory is never achieved. For example, the person who works out at the gym seven days a week, and this person continues saying that the muscles are never big enough – even though to the eyes of the beholder the muscles are huge.

It seems to me that in order to have a healthy measurement of success, one must first evaluate the understanding of the concept of enough. It is important to create a reasonable and healthy parameter of what enough would look like given the cards we have been dealt.

I define success in direct relationship to accomplishing goals at a professional and personal level with a realistic and clearly defined 'enough' end point that correlates with my intellectual and physical abilities to carry on my desired goals. If in the process I make more money than what I need to live a humble and comfortable life, the merrier. However, in all of my entrepreneurships and activities making money was never the end goal.

Off till the next walk!

Advice Not Taken

The frustration crawls inside your veins when you know your advice is sound and the best choice for the person you are suggesting it. For reasons of stubbornness, closed mind syndrome, or plane rebelliousness the person persists in doing things in a way that are either detrimental to that person's well-being, the environment, or to others.

I have friends whose parents are in their upper 80s. The parents refuse to do what it is suggested to them. One of my friends was heart-broken because his father was doing whatever rather than following the plan my friend had put in place – pills in a container so the father knew what to take and when, a helper to do the shopping, cleaning, and ensure the pills were taken. Father decided to let the helper go, and not to take the pills because he knew better.

I have an amazing son to whom I advise to eat a more balance diet, sleep longer hours, and read more. I was feeling that maybe the way my message was being passed was the problem. I changed the way of communication emulating the marketing techniques of those who are very good at making you buy their products. It did not work either!

I then realized that advice is like a gift – once you give it, you no longer own it, and the receiving party is entitled to do whatever they please with it. I am sure you have been in a situation where you spend hours thinking of the perfect gift, and you probably spent a good amount of money to acquire it, however, the recipient of the gift does not care much about it.

I also do not like to repeat myself. If you tell me of a problem, I ask if you would like ideas for potential solutions. You say yes and I use my valuable time for that. Then, you do not follow the plan because it requires change, and change is often hard. Then, do not come back later whining about the same problem again. I have already provided a solution. What do you expect? A different outcome while doing exactly the same? Albert Einstein called that madness.

Off till the next walk!

Regrets

I have none. Every decision and choice I made were done to the best of my knowledge, my capabilities, and the tools I had at hand.

One cannot prove a negative. I cannot say that if I had done D instead of A or B, the outcome would have been different because we cannot undo the past, rewind the whole situation as if it were a movie, and change one of the variables to see if the outcome would have been different in a more or less favorable way. Thus, in following my Buddhist philosophy of life, there is no point in regurgitating the past and creating emotions about things that are already gone. When I ruminate about the past, it is to state what it was, as in some of the stories you have read here, or to create a lesson-learned scenario to ensure the present decision will have a more desirable outcome.

Have you seen the movie Under the Tuscan Sun? Francesca rushes to the town of Positano to surprise Marcelo. She finds him with another woman. The same situation happened to me. At the time, smartphones were not available. Today, thanks to the smartphone, we can speak with a person regardless of where that person is at the moment. My lesson learned is that those surprises can backfire. It is better to have a chat on the phone before showing up uninvited.

One of my favorite songs was written by Charles Gaston Dumont and Michel Jacques Pierre Vaucaire for French singer Edith Piaf. The song goes "no, nothing at all. No, I do not regret anything. [...] Neither evil, I don't care at all. [...] It is paid, swept away, forgotten. I do not care about the past."

I do remember the past experiences - the good, the bad, and the ugly — with a frame of mind that does not include the emotion of regret or anger or sadness. I pass those memories in my mind with the motto of 'what it was, was; what it is, is.'

It would be impossible to live a life to its full potential if one has to carry a heavy anchor of regrets tied to the waist. The concept of lessons learned seems to be more beneficial to help not to repeat a situation whose outcome was not the most desirable when we observe the situation again several years later.

Thanks to the teachings of Buddha and my grandmother, my decisions went through an array of check marks — legal, ethically correct, morally acceptable to our Western standards, right intention, right understanding, right livelihood. Do I have the needed tools — money, time, skills, environment — to ensure the success of the decision or choice? If the ideal tools are not present and the decision must be made, how can I combine resources to do the best possible outcome given the tools and conditions of the environment?

Once the plan is laid and executed, it is like the water that flows along a river — you cannot force it back and make it reflow again. You feel peace of mind because you know you made the right effort to make the best decision or choice given the circumstances.

This topic of regrets is very important because I know many individuals who walk through the present carrying a load of regrets. When I decided to write these stories, my hope was that I could also help you, the reader, embrace a philosophy of life that allows you to unload the burdens of the past. Some of the stories are entertaining, and others, like this one, will require that you put the book aside for a moment and reflect on what you have just read.

Do you carry regrets with you? Can you deconstruct them? By deconstructing the regret, I mean that you state what you regret first. Then, you have to make a list of the conditions that were surrounding you at the time you made the decision that today you are regretting. Then, you need to find what variable you would have needed to know at the time so you could have made a different decision. This is the variable that is weighing heavily on your mind. You find yourself repeating "if I would have had" or "if I would have known."

Read again the paragraph above where I say that I also showed up unannounced to the house of whom I thought was a serious relationship to find him with another woman. I was shocked. I said a few "parole cattive"[3] and moved on. Did I feel sad,

---

[3] Bad words in Italian

cheated, deceived, humiliated and used? Yes, of course! Did those feelings linger more than the time it took me to arrive home? Nope. It was like the thought that enters your mind while you are meditating. We acknowledge the thought, and we move on back to the focus on the sensation of the breath coming in and out.

Off till the next walk!

Cooper is Gone

I bought my green Mini Cooper in May 2004. It was one of the first imported into the United States. I baptized it with a license plate ALOSP2 which, fully spelled, reads "a los pedos." This is an Argentinean expression that people use all the time when they are very busy and doing things very fast, one task after the other without time to stop not even to look at themselves in the mirror. It could translate in English as zoom-zoom.

When I bought the Mini Cooper, I was teaching at a three-letter agency in San Diego, and one of my students, Jake, asked me if he could take the Cooper for a spin. I said yes without knowing that Jake had a reputation for being crazy behind the wheel. He put the Cooper on I-15 North and the next thing I know, we are driving at 120 mph! I thought "well, if we get stopped by the police, he is the one with the badge and the one behind the wheel."

In January 2005, I moved to Virginia and Cooper went with me. After a few months in the city, and feeling like a cat inside a box, I purchased a 4-acre split ranch in Fredericksburg, VA, and Cooper and I were delighted to be in the countryside.

In Virginia, one needs to have at least three individuals in the vehicle to drive in the fast lane. There are parking lots with the famous "slug lines," people standing in line waiting for the next car to jump into. Because one usually drives by the slug lane at the same time every day, it is common to give a ride to the same person every day. However, one day, a very large man was next in line. I tried to explain in polite terms that I did not think he was going to fit in the back seat of lovely Cooper. He insisted, and off we went along the freeway doing wheelies with the Cooper because I truly felt that my front wheels were up in the air.

Mon son, Dakota, Cooper and I

Pirate, my Harlequin Great Dane, liked to ride in the front seat. On nice weather days, I would open the sunroof and whenever I would stop at a traffic light, Pirate always wanted to stick his head out of the sunroof as if he were a periscope. One day, I was standing in line at the local supermarket and two ladies were chatting in line in front of me.

One said to the other, "you will not believe what I saw yesterday! This lady in a Mini Cooper with a giant Great Dane head sticking out of the sunroof!" The other lady started laughing. I felt obliged to tap her on the shoulder and tell her that I was the lady in the Cooper. The funniest thing is that she recognized me because the day before I had waved at her when she was looking at us with that face of consternation that people put when they are not sure whether they are or aren't tripping.

When my son turned 10, he wanted to drive the Cooper. I put the horse, the dogs and the cats away as a measure of precaution. I spent a good amount of time giving him very detailed explanations on how to drive the amazing Mini Cooper. I put my son behind the wheel, and I sat on the passenger side. He started driving in circles in the front acre of the property. In the beginning, he was going slowly, doing circles around the trees, and making a nice square route on the property. Fifteen minutes later, he was feeling very confident, and he increased the speed, and the design of his route. I got a call from my neighbor asking whether I was feeling well. I said, "I am feeling very well. I am having fun teaching my son how to drive." He politely suggested that he was concerned about my state of mind when he looked through his window and saw the Cooper doing crazy pirouettes on my front yard.

After a while, it was time for me to return to my lovely California. I came by air, and Cooper arrived on the bed of a towing truck. Once I settled in my new place, I bought an Akita who got used to riding in the back of the Cooper. I had folded the backseats to convert the always handy Cooper into a mini, super mini truck.

My son was going to a private high school, and since I was self-employed here in California, it was easy for me to pick up the kids after school. Ernie would take our son and two of his friends to school in the morning on his way to work, and I would pick up the three kids in the afternoon. This particular high school has a large body of wealthy students who live in Mexico, and come to San Diego to attend the private school. One day, it dawned on my son to ask what the license plate of the Cooper meant. He had asked about it when he was a kid but now he was more self-conscious of what others would think of his mother showing up to pick him up with a license plate that had the word "pedos" (farts). He told me, "I do not want to ride in a car that says 'Go Farts'." He thought the license plate meant a cheering slogan like "Go [Football Team of your choice]." It took a lot of dialog to explain that it was an Argentinean expression that few would figure out if they were from another Spanish speaking country, and that it means zoom zoom. Finally, he was at ease about riding with his friends in the "farting" Cooper.

In 2015, I flew to Germany to buy a German Shepherd Dog who also learned to ride in the back of the Cooper along with Luna – the Akita. For three years, the Akita, the GSD and I were happy traveling everywhere and anywhere there was a great spot for us to hike.

In 2018, Cooper was suffering the aches and pains that come with age, and it was getting too expensive to repair. I decommissioned it hoping that one day I was going to find either a boyfriend who knew how to fix cars or earn the large amount of money needed to repair the wear and tear in the engine, and the inside.

In December 2021, I had the Cooper parked in the driveway, and I felt he was begging to ride again. In the absence of a boyfriend with mechanic skills, and the funds to repair it, I called my friend Michael W., who is always involved in off-road racing, and loves to work on engines, to tell him that Santa Claus had left a present for him in my driveway. He picked it up in February 2022, and I am delighted that awesome Cooper will now live in the home of a friend, and roar again on the roads of California.

Off till the next walk!

Friendships

When I meet a new person, who tries to befriend me, I am always curious to find out how many friends that person has kept from childhood, adolescence and/or college years.

Friends, and the length of time they have remained in your life, can be compared to richness and wealth. A person can be rich in friends. These are the friends that last a short time because this person has a selfish personality and/or other unwholesome traits. On the other hand, a person can have a wealth of friends. These are the friends from childhood, adolescence and college that have remained in the life of this individual, as well as friends that were created later in life and passed the 5-year mark.

A person rich in friends has many, however, the fabric that holds them is thin. There is always the quid pro quo in between them. Favors are done in exchange of favors rather than for the compassionate sake of helping a friend.

A person with a wealth of friends might be able to count them with two hands, however, the fabric that holds these friendships is strong. These are the friends that lend a hand without wondering what they can get in return.

I am fortunate to have a wealth of friends. You will read the name of most of them in the Acknowledgement section of this book. There is

After the Walk

only room to acknowledge a few throughout this book, nevertheless, to the rest of my friends that I hold so closely to my heart, you know who you are.

Off till next walk!

Transplantation

A few weeks ago, I created the painting titled "Waiting for Pablo U." The painting is a self-portrait from the time I was in my very early 20s.

Waiting for Pablo U (2022)

I went to live in Lago Gutierrez in the Patagonia region of Argentina, and I fell in love with a guy, who is a few years older than me, named Pablo U. He was managing a local pub while he was figuring out whether to return to his life and ex-girlfriend in Buenos Aires, or remain in Patagonia.

We dated while he was trying to figure that out, and I moved in with him. The pub was in a gorgeous cabaña with many rooms that were used as living quarters. It had a giant fireplace that would keep us warm and cozy during those very cold days. The winters in Patagonia are no joke.

I fell in love with Pablo and the dog Franca. I guess I watched too many movies where this one girl is so irresistible that changes the life of anyone. Based on his attitude, I felt I was that one girl.

We went everywhere together. We cooked together. We were both avid readers, and it was such a joy to be reading books with my legs wrapped around his, Franca by our side, in front of the fireplace. When I close my eyes, and take a deep breath, I can remember the smell of the whole place.

During the night, the room would get freezing cold, and we were using a cow hide to keep us warm. Franca was always sleeping by our feet and at times competing for the warmest side of the bed.

Unfortunately, and to my surprise, one day, he told me that the ex-girlfriend was arriving in a week, and I had to move out from his place. Just like that, and as cold as the Patagonia winter.

An Australian couple, who was living just four blocks from the Pub, let me stay at their spare room while I was finding another home to rent. During the two weeks I lived with John Edmunds, his wife and three adorable children, I spent hours sitting at the window Waiting for Pablo U —ergo, the tittle of the painting.

The Edmunds had a simple but beautiful home at the edge of the lake. John was lecturing me in philosophy and stoicism. I was young, and madly in love. I had to consolidate the teaching of the Buddha about non-attachment, and the teachings of the Stoics that John was pushing full throttle into my head.

San Carlos de Bariloche

Several weeks passed, and Pablo never came to grab me by the waist, lift me up high and tell me that he was also in love with me, like in the movies. I found another beautiful home to rent just three blocks from the Edmunds. A few months later, it was my turn to leave Patagonia for a different pasture.

In 2022, after I finished the painting, I decided to take advantage of the power of social media to allow people to find others regardless of the many miles in between. I found the famous Pablo U. He gladly remembered me, and I showed him the painting and the write-up about it that I had posted on social media. He said he was left speechless. He also shared a recent photo of his, and he remains as handsome as always.

After walking the dogs, I thought of the concept of transplantation. I thought of the few guys with whom I had fallen crazily in love. Even if I would think about the possibility of going back to any of my previous loves, and if that guy would be willing to restart the romance again, they all live abroad.

I am not willing to move where they are. My life is here. They also have well-established lives where they are. It would be like transplanting a well-established tree. The tree will go into shock, and it would die in the process.

I imagine the old tree missing the birds that were visiting it in the old location, and the worms that were caressing its roots. The many dogs that day in and day out were stopping to say hello to the tree by politely lifting their legs against the tree, and gifting its roots the infallible yellow stream.

I put myself in the roots of the tree, and I do not think I would survive. When we and plants are young, the transplantation process is easier. We are more malleable, and adaptation to a new environment is possible. We have the strength of the youth to grow new branches, create new opportunities, set roots deeper in the new place, and sustain change.

This has nothing to do with age. It has to do with how well and deeply our roots have been established in the land where we currently are. When I open my arms here in California, and my feet touch the ground, as if I were a tree, I know the kind of birds that can land on me. I know the kind of worms and gophers that will be messing with my roots.

For this reason, I do not think it is feasibly to rekindle the loves that are now in faraway lands from us.

An old friend of mine once told me "never go back to the place where once you were so happy."

Off till the next walk!

Fireplaces

The temperature was in the low 30s this morning when I started walking the dogs. We could see the steam coming out of our mouths. The dogs were accelerating the pace of the walk knowing that it was going to warm us faster. I was trailing behind them when I caught the first whiff of burnt wood.

The houses around the park were burning wood in their fireplaces and, after the walk, I thought of all the places I have lived that had a fireplace. A simple feature of a home, used for centuries to warm all sentient beings, it has the power of keeping us mesmerized with the changing colors of the flames burning the wood.

Fireplaces are also associated with romance, celebration of Christmas, a place where families would sit in front of and tell stories to their children. A fireplace, for me, it is like an object that spits out heat and wisdom.

There was a fireplace in all the houses where I grew up, in the house I moved in with my ex-husband, the house I bought after the divorce, the house in Virginia, the house I rented in San Diego when I returned from Virginia, and the house I own now in California. Let's not forget the fireplace of the Patagonia house I described in the previous story.

Who has not made love in front of a fireplace? Enjoyed a good wine while being held in the arms of a loved one? Read a good book in front of it? Spent a long time letting the mind wonder aimlessly while enjoying the dances the flame plays with the burning wood?

Close your eyes and try to image one of the fireplaces of your life.

Off till the next walk!

Caught on my Phone

At the park across from my house, there is a beautiful tennis court with signs on both sides of the entrance that clearly read "NO DOGS ALLOWED ON ATHLETIC COURT."

Kapa'a and I were enjoying our morning walk and training when I saw four individuals and two dogs inside the athletic court. I pulled my phone out in video mode and politely asked if they could read the sign. I always talk about the pitfall of assuming things so I was not going to assume that these four individuals could read. The following is the dialog caught on my video:

> Me: Excuse me, can you read the sign?
>
> Man: Yes, we are taking them out now.
>
> Woman: Yes, we are about to take them out now.
>
> Me: Well, you should not put them in at all. That is why we have the sign.

I continued walking and I encountered them again outside of the athletic court on their way home. The lady holding a Husky said "I do not like being on your phone," to which I replied "This is a public place. If you do not like being on people's phones, then do not break the rules by putting your dogs on an athletic court, and having the nerve of standing inside the court, right next to the sign that reads no dogs allowed."

This is not the first time I catch people using the athletic court as a kennel run for their dogs. The last time happened on Christmas day. Six dogs inside the athletic court, and four people with them. The dialog on that occasion was belligerent on their part. One of the men started calling me racist and that if they would have been white I would not have said anything. It amazes me that even though he was the one doing the wrong thing, and instead of admitting he had willingly trespassed in an area he was not supposed to be, he opted for what these days has become the nonsense insult of the day – calling someone a racist.

Besides being cheap, it delegitimizes the actual cases of racism that do in fact exist all over the world.

I am not a Karen. I do not care who you are, what you look like, etc., etc. – if you are putting

After the Walk

dogs in the athletic court, you will end up on my phone and then with the park ranger. Period the end.

Off till the next walk!

Coronado Bridge

Before the walk, I read a beautiful message sent by Dr. Peter Attia about the Golden Gate Bridge in San Francisco in relation to its beauty and the fact that it is also the preferred bridge for jumpers.

In his message, he talks about the jump prevention barrier that is being constructed on the bridge since 2018, and it will be finished in 2023. He makes a very good point about the determination to end one's life, and points to data, from experiments conducted by Berkeley researcher Richard Seiden and others, that show that suicide behavior could be a momentary lapse of reason.

In San Diego County, we have the famous Coronado Bridge which opened in 1969. In November 2021, Diane Bell wrote a column[4] for the San Diego Union Tribune about the Coronado Bridge jumpers – two who survived. It is estimated that more than 400 individuals have jumped from this bridge.

The Coronado Bridge has a suicide prevention sign with a phone number to call. The irony is that at that exact place, and in most parts of the bridge,

---

4

https://www.sandiegouniontribune.com/columnists/story/2021-11-09/column-coronado-bridge-tells-suicide-story accessed on February 2022.

cellular reception is nonexistent and at best very weak and spotty.

Here is a reminder again that help is available at the National Suicide Prevention Lifeline at 1-800-273-8255.

Remember that now it has been proven that suicide behavior is momentary, and even though you might think that there is absolutely no solution to your problem, your mind is operating at a limited capacity and in a narrow channel. The amazing men and women working at the NSPL will help you see with clarity the next minute in your life, the next hour in your life where you will be able to see the light at the end of the tunnel until you reach a professional that can help you move on.

We have made incredible advances in technology and in the field of cognitive behavioral psychology. I propose the government should fund, through the National Suicide Prevention Lifeline, necklace alert devices that are freely distributed to those at risk of suicide. Almost daily, we read in the newspapers and social media posts about the high rate of suicides among the veteran population. This group should be the first one to receive the necklace. It can be discreetly worn underneath clothing. Because we now know that the suicide behavior is momentary, one click on that button could save a life. Once the person clicks on the button, a call automatically enters the person's cellphone, family members listed on the emergency list get a call, and, of course, EMT personnel who specialize in dealing with these types of emergencies.

A friend once told me that he thought the act of committing suicide is the most selfish act a person can do because of the sadness he causes to those who are left behind. I do not agree that at the moment an individual is contemplating suicide, we can say that the person has the clarity of mind to think that the act about to be committed is selfish, and because of that awareness the person backs down from suicide.

By nature, all species strive to preserve life. In fact, sometimes we have called selfish those who in situations of emergency run to save their own lives rather than execute an act of heroism in saving other's lives even to the potential risk to them.

As I write this chapter, the news media informs the world about the death by suicide of a female model who was only 30 years old and, in the eyes of the beholder, she had it all. However, I can imagine her feeling the pain and anguish deeply inside.

Off to the next walk!

Earthquakes

We were walking when the dogs and I felt the earth shaking below us. I realized we were having a minor earthquake, although enough for us to feel it under our feet. We continued walking and after the walk I began thinking of all the earthquakes I have endured.

The Algarrobo earthquake in Chile that killed 82 people was also very much felt in Buenos Aires, Argentina. My brother and I were living on the 24th floor of a luxury apartment building in Belgrano R. Suddenly, while we were having dinner, I felt nauseous. I thought the food might be spoiled. As I was telling my brother that I was feeling dizzy, we saw the lamp moving from side to side, and soon after the whole building. We had tickets to the theater so we decided to grab the tickets and rush down the stairs as fast as we could. The whole building was moving at least a foot from side to side.

My first California earthquake took place while I was shopping at a super market looking for toothpaste. Suddenly, all of them began falling from the shelves. I thought I was developing some magic or exorcism powers. One of the employees screamed the word earthquake and I rushed out of the store like a bat out of hell.

In 1994, I was married, and my husband and I were enjoying a weekend at the Ritz Carlton Hotel in Dana Point, California. Ernie always wanted upstairs bedrooms, however, the hotel made a mistake that day and gave us a downstairs room. All the upstairs bedrooms were booked.

During the afternoon, we were relaxing by the pool when suddenly one of the employees started rushing everybody out of the water. We grew a little concerned so we asked another employee what the matter was. He pointed at a giant brown turd floating in the pristine blue waters of the pool. A child decided that it was the perfect giant toilet to dump one.

The saying goes who is counting but, in my mind, I was counting the mishaps – the wrong room, and then the dirty pool.

At 4 a.m., Ernie woke me up saying "Ceci, we are having a little earthquake." When I opened my eyes, the shutters in the room were sounding like flamenco castanets. The bed was shaking. The whole room felt as if I were inside a blender. I grabbed my robe, Ernie's hand, and we both jumped from the -lucky for us – first floor balcony onto the grass where there were already many frightened souls looking at the hotel. They probably were wondering whether the building was going to crumble down in front of us.

In August 1998, our son was 9-months old when our house was shaken by the San Andreas fault. We both rushed to his bedroom, and stood under the door frame. We had built his crib under an earthquake protection type of wooden structure, so he was completely safe and asleep. He did not even realize that his parents were petrified a few feet from him.

In 2011, I was living in Virginia, and the idea of an earthquake was so removed from my mind that when the Mineral Earthquake made me fall down the stairs of my home, I thought a massive explosion had taken place in Quantico. The dogs were howling. The cats rushed out of the house. I rushed out of the house and went to talk to my neighbor who was also frantic wondering what the explosion we heard was all about.

During the past three months, we have had several earthquakes in Southern California. On the biggest one I felt, my dog Juliette began barking at the same time I felt my bed shaking. I thought I had someone inside the home. It took my brain a few seconds to realize we were having another bloody earthquake.

As I was pondering on all this moving of the earth, I thought of all the other natural disasters such as hurricanes, tornados, fires, and floods. I take the earthquake any time over those other four.

Off till the next walk!

Commercialization of Mindfulness

I am mesmerized, and disappointed at the same time, that one of the eight tenets of the Eightfold Path of the Buddha's philosophy is being commercialized, and people are making an industry of that.

Actually, I should not be surprised because, after all, we live under a capitalism system where many ideas flourish to the marketplace. Some are good. Some are bad. Last year, the American reality TV star Stephanie Matto announced that she was selling her farts in a jar for $1000 a jar.

In a country where people are willing to pay any amount of money to have farts in a jar, then, I am not surprised that someone thought of making money from one of the tenets of the Eightfold Path.

These companies and individuals offering mindfulness courses that promise a panacea of mental change, and success, and who knows what else, remind me of the snake-oil salesmen of the Old West.

For the Christians reading my book, can you imagine if someone grabs one of the Ten Commandments and begins selling courses and promising life changes, etc. just by narrowly focusing on that one Commandment?

I have a friend, Crawford Coates, who wrote a book about mindfulness for emergency and law enforcement personnel. I understand what he is trying to accomplish, and I also agree with him that if he were to even suggest the Buddha's philosophy as a whole to this group, he would be shut down immediately. Nobody would pay any attention to what he has to say. However, he has skillfully incorporated in his book all the other seven tenets of the Eightfold Path. He even invited me to talk on his podcast about mindfulness from the point of view of a Westerner who was educated as a Zen Buddhist. He is certainly not a snake-oil salesman, and his program will save lives in the EMT and law enforcement communities.

If I were to commercialize one of the tenets to improve the quality of life of many, it would be the Right Speech tenet. Since 2016, the level of vitriolic exchange of words has escalated in all spheres of society – Congress, industry, Hollywood, sports, and schools. If you want to take an accelerated course on vitriolic dialog, spend 10 minutes scrolling through Twitter.

What is Right Speech? It is when you talk and state facts without cutting a hole in the soul of other sentient beings. For example, if you are having an argument with a spouse, colleague, child, etc., instead of saying "you are an asshole," you would say "you are behaving as those type of individuals who are often called assholes."

Imagine a pristine and newly painted wall in your home. Someone comes and punches the wall and makes a hole. You patch the hole using some type of putty and you paint it again. However, the hole on that wall is permanent even if you do not see it with your naked eye because you did a good job at repairing it well. The truth is that the hole will be in that wood forever.

When you call someone an unflattering adjective, you are making a hole in the soul of that person. It does not matter how profusely you apologize afterwards, the damage has already been done, and it is permanent.

I see people offering mindfulness courses to cure anxiety disorders, among other things. Since I have an anxiety disorder, and I am a Buddhist, someone asked me a long time ago what kind of a Buddhist I was that still had an anxiety disorder. I laughed. Then, I explained, with all the Buddha patience, that an anxiety disorder is a chemical unbalance that develops without the sufferer having any doing in it. You are born with a brain that lacks the capability to properly absorb serotonin. The Buddhist philosophy helped me enormously in dealing with that. While a person suffering from an anxiety disorder is in the middle of a panic attack, the Buddhist philosophy, and in particular the teachings of Thich Nhat Hanh about focusing on the breath, are instrumental in helping us navigate to the other end of the panic attack.

If I were to put my panic attacks in the form of art, a painting in my case, I see a giant wave that I begin climbing up as the panic attack begins to form. Once I am at the crest of the wave, the panic attack is in full blown mode, and I begin to experience the physical symptoms that accompany the typical panic attack —heart beats faster, dizziness, lack of 3D perception and an array that other symptoms that some people experience. Then, I surf down the wave as I regain control, and the panic attack is going away.

Buddhist philosophy and my breathing practice have helped me surf this wave feeling that I am under control of the situation. I would say that I am surfing in a less panicky way.

Whatever it is that you are suffering from at an emotional level, I highly encourage you to read on your own the hundreds of books written by Thich Nhat Hanh. You do not need to suddenly become a Buddhist. You do not need to abandon whatever religion you practice because Zen Buddhism is not a religion. It is a philosophy of life. You can learn to practice the Eightfold Path to have a much more fulfilling life while at the same time you continue with whatever religion you practice.

Above all, you do not need to buy expensive snake-oil.

Off till the next walk!

Not Good Enough

On the chapter of Free Money, I talked about a concept Morgan Housel described in his Psychology of Money, people who lack the concept of enough, meaning that they never feel satisfied. They want more and more, and they are willing to disregard law and ethics to attain that more and more.

How about the concept of enough when others tell us that whatever we do is not good enough? You do an act of kindness, however, the person receiving your kindness complains that it is too short.

I thought about those who judge us on whatever we do, and for them, it is never good enough.

My father was one of those individuals. I could win a regatta; however, instead of hearing words such as "congratulations, well done!," he would say "too bad the sailboat behind you was that close." I would get the highest grade on a class, and I would hear "too bad on the other one you were a few points below."

I was fortunate to have an amazing grandmother and mentors who recognized my accomplishments, and gave me the courage to keep going, and the self-confidence to ignore those who were unable to appreciate my gains.

I do not have a feeling of resentment toward my father. I am stating what it was. However, I wondered whether this exposure to the "not good enough" attitude from a father pushed me toward the eclectic personal and professional life I developed in early adulthood. Maybe, if there is a psychologist reading this book, I will one day read the answer in a social media post.

The activities I have pursued, I have done them always employing Right Effort, another tenet of the Eightfold Path. I have always striven to do my best. I have been fortunate that, in adulthood, I have received recognition for my jobs well-done from colleagues, friends, and family. In the areas where I needed improvement, they would suggest that, and I would work on the improvement.

I have a funny story about a family member suggesting an improvement. A few chapters earlier, I explained about the "slug line" in Virginia. One day, my son, who at the time of this story was 7 years old, was riding with me in the car, and the person sitting in the passenger seat asked me how many languages I spoke. I replied by saying "French, Italian, Portuguese, Spanish, and English with an accent." My sassy child said "Ah ah missy, you need a lot of help with the English." We all broke into a loud and long laughter.

Off till the next walk!

Don't Mix the Boxes

Our lives take place in different scenarios and realms, such as work, the family network, the school network, relationships, health, friends, people we encounter at random, the gym or club where we practice a physical activity, finances, raising children, etc.

I like to call these realms "the boxes of life." Each one of these boxes comes packed with its own dynamic, pleasures, and dramas, things that you can control, and things that are beyond your control. For the boxes that come with other people in them, such as work and a gym or club, you need to truly master the art of patience, and to learn when you engage or continue to focus with the activity that it is directly under your nose.

At work, you are required to maintain certain behaviors and sometimes to swallow your thoughts instead of telling bosses or co-workers to go "foxtrotting" themselves because you know the consequences are termination, and loss of income. Situations like this create stress. If you have not developed a healthy channel to release that stress, you often carry it onto the other boxes, such as your health box and/or your family box.

This stress carried onto the relationships, children, pets, or family boxes can lead to your snapping at them, hitting the pet, hitting the children, screaming, excessive drinking, etc. None of the members of these boxes have done anything wrong to you, and there is no reason for you to take your frustration and/or anger accumulated at work onto them. The Health box also gets affected because the saying goes that stress kills.

In fact, the point of this story is to teach you that what happens in one box, should be dealt with and kept in that box. Something to the extent of the famous saying "what happens in Las Vegas, stays buried in the desert."

How about driving and encountering a collection of knuckleheads that cut in front of you? You arrive to your destination with all your muscles in a knot because the stress is consuming you. Then, you lash out to whoever is the first one you encounter.

Do you bring your work problems into your personal life? You arrive home from work after having a rough day, and you treat everybody at home rudely, and your excuse is that you had a bad day at work.

Are you having problems at home with children, spouse, relatives? Then, you arrive at work, and everybody has to put up with your lack of consideration, bad manners, etc., and your excuse is that things are not going that well at home.

If these scenarios describe you, then it is time for you to learn about the boxes of life, and how to compartmentalize each one of them.

The figure below shows some of the cubes we encounter in life. I left two blanks intentionally so you can add any other environment you navigate in life, and that it is not already mentioned here.

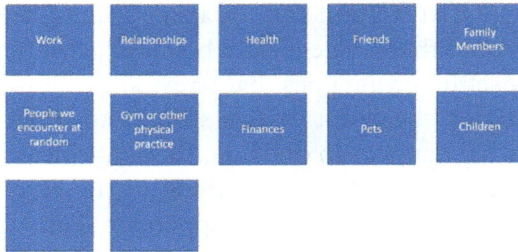

Work	Relationships	Health	Friends	Family Members
People we encounter at random	Gym or other physical practice	Finances	Pets	Children

How do you fix this? You must deal with the problems you encounter in each one of these boxes within the box itself. If there are problems at work, go to HR department if needed, or kindly ask a co-worker to stop doing whatever that person does that bothers you. When you leave work, leave the feelings that arose in the work place there.

When you arrive home, whether it is a peaceful or also a stressful environment, be present in the moment of the feelings that belong to that place exclusively. Do not bring in the feelings created at work, or when some knucklehead cut you off on the freeway.

In other words, do not poison one well with the nasty waters of another.

I am aware and understand that you might want to talk with your spouse, or friends, about what it is going on in the work box, or any other box. I am not saying that you cannot have a conversation about events that took place at work, or while you were driving, or in any of the other boxes. I am asking you to check the negative emotions inside the box where they took place. When you come home, and your spouse asks how your day went, you can state the overall picture, such as the project is going well, however, I am having problems with boss, or coworker, and leave the conversation at that. Even if your spouse asks for details, do not relive again the stressful emotions of the work box into the family box.

In life, when an event occurs, we can control 90% of it. The 10% that we cannot control, we must accept it. In Zen Buddhism, we say "what it is, is" and we leave it at that. For the 90% we can control, we apply the Eightfold Path tenets to ensure that we speak with kindness, we understand the other sentient beings, we do the right action with the right intention, we are mindful and present in the moment, we choose right livelihood, we put right effort on all we do, and we practice concentration, paying attention to our breathing.

Off till the next walk!

Support Living Artists

The dead artists don't need to make ends meet.

Besides working with the dogs, and cyber defense and analysis, I am also a fine artist. You can find my paintings at www.ceciliaanastos.com.

A few months ago, I typed the phrase "support the living artists" on a search engine, and I discovered many interesting posts, including advertising for t-shirts sold online with the legend "Support the living artists – the dead don't need to eat."

During today's walk, for a moment, I got lost in the beautiful light of Collier Park, and I thought that one of these days I was going to do a painting of it. Then, before going back to my breathing during the walk, I thought what else I could do to find buyers of my paintings.

I understand that you might like art movements from the past. I do as well. My favorite periods are Impressionism and post-Impressionism. For the past, we have museums, such as the Musée d'Orsai in Paris with an amazing collection of painters from these two movements. In San Diego, I enjoy going to Balboa Park, and visit the many art museums we have there as well.

At home, I have many paintings from living Belgium painter Guy Moreaux, and living Australian painter Cindy Parsley, and, of course, some of my own. Although I have two reproductions from the dead French painter William-Adolphe Bouguereau, I did not buy them, someone gifted them to me. I would never buy a print, or reproduction, and spend a cent in framing it because I truly believe in supporting the living artists.

Of course, you might think that this statement is a self-serving purpose. It would be if I have not bought paintings from other living artists, but I did. I own eight Moreauxes!

These are some of the reasons why I want to help push this movement of supporting the living artists, besides the fact that the dead ones do not need the money, many did not leave descendants that would enjoy the profit of their posthumous sales, and auction houses are the ones that get the most from the sale of dead painters' works.

I list the reasons below:

Art is an investment – If you buy from an artist that, like myself, participates in juried exhibitions, and receives awards, then your painting will increase in value. A painting will either maintain its original value or increase it. It will not decrease its value.

If you buy from a local artist, you are helping the local economy. Artists pay a lot of taxes each time we sell a painting, and those taxes go to support the local library, schools, road projects, etc.

When you hang the painting of a living artist on your wall, you can almost feel the story that inspired that painting. All of my paintings come with a Certificate of Authenticity that describes the inspiration, or raison d'être, for that particular painting.

There are many forgeries being sold in the art markets, and even experts sometimes have a difficult time asserting the authenticity of a painting. When you buy from a living artist that provides a certificate of authenticity, you are receiving an indisputable proof for that painting.

When you buy a unique and original painting rather than a print or a reproduction, you are hanging something that nobody else has. This is the reason why my paintings are not available in print. I only sell the original so the owners of my paintings feel special because they have one of a kind.

When you buy the works from living artists, you are helping advance the future of the art world. I understand if you want to own a Picasso or a Pollock. If you can afford it, go for it, as long as you buy the original. At the same time, I would like to see in your home some paintings from a living artist as well. This way, you balance the scale. You also impact the career of the living artist.

I hope that you find these reasons compelling to go peruse my website, www.cecilianastos.com, and hang one. or more. of my paintings on your walls.

Off till the next walk!

Happiness

I am very active in the social media platform LinkedIn, and, in the last few weeks, several of my connections brought up the subject of happiness. I was reading Harari's Homo Deus book where he addresses this same topic in the first few pages of the book. I read a few of those posts before the walk, and, for a moment during the walk, I thought about my happiness.

Happiness cannot be bought, acquired by osmosis, and/or suddenly found when you meet someone new. Happiness does not come from external events and/or possessions. True happiness is present inside yourself. If you are walking through life saying that you will be happy the day that you [win the lotto, find the perfect partner, get the job x]; in other words, expecting that external factors will bring you happiness, you will probably live without satisfaction.

I believe that happiness comes from my inner self. You might wonder how you find the seed of happiness inside you to make it grow and let it become the essence of your being. I recommend that you start looking for the most basic, focus on your breathing. Breathing, in particular during the pandemic we are going through, is a luxury that as of this writing 3 million individuals do not have the pleasure to continue doing. Take a deep breath, and smile. That smile is watering the seed of happiness.

Do external events affect me? Yes, of course. However, they do not erode my natural state of happiness. They act like icing on a cake. You could have the most amazing cake, and add some icing that gives an awkward flavor or one that enhances the flavor of the cake. Nevertheless, the amazing cake remains the same. I have experienced loss, anxiety, fear, passion, and crazy love... all these were icings on my cake of happiness.

In French, we have an expression that says *état de bonheur permanent.* This is how I live my life.

Want to learn more about this philosophy? I recommend following the late Zen Buddhist monk Thich Nhat Hanh's writings and his Plum Village Monastery in France.

Off till the next walk!

Breaking Ground

I have been watching the TV series titled 1883, and I realized during this walk how many things I have accomplished while breaking ground in areas where things had never been done before, and pushing away customs in some of the most conservative environments I have been.

While watching this series, I see myself as Elsa Dutton, portrayed by Isabel May, embracing freedom full throttle.

My journey began when I turned 8 years old, and I was the only girl participating at the regattas of the class Optimist at the club I belonged to. When I turned 12, I became the captain of the team. There was a lot of bullying involved by some of the guys who were not happy that "a skirt was leading the team." I shrugged it all. I think it made me stronger. I had Cristina Lawrence, my grandma, and my parents having my back. The others did not matter.

When I turned 18, I introduced the famous Brazilian thong bikini to the club. One of the most conservative yachting clubs in the country, and there I was proudly showing my awesome buttocks "a la Brazil." Yeap... all eyes on me with such a glaze that I was feeling the burning on my behind. Six months later, Mariana B., another young gal who did not participate in the regattas but was always sun bathing at the club, shows up with her own thong bikini.

Within a few months, the same ladies that were watching Mariana and me in horror decided to sport their own thong bathing suits. Maybe they got tired that their husbands were too busy watching somewhere else.

In the 90s, I broke ground at the Del Mar Polo Club with my cavalletti and massage techniques to recover polo ponies after injuries, and to prevent them from getting injuries in the first place. I will always be grateful to Suzanne G., and Brian M. for trusting my speech, and giving me a horse to show them what I could do. After that, I was looking like Mother Teresa whenever I would pull into the polo club, I had many clients, and horses lined up to enjoy the ability of my skills, and my skillful cavalletti techniques. Did I hear jokes from the players? Of course! The most common one was if I also did massage on people. I would tell them "no because men do not buck." That would leave them mouth opened, and perplexed, because they could not figure out what the quick reply could be. By the time they were catching their breath, I was gone with the horse.

I broke ground in the areas of OSINT and cyber defense, but that will be a subject of another book, maybe.

If I would have lived in 1883, I would have been an Elsa Dutton through and through.

Off till the next walk!

Reincarnation

Today, during the walk, I got a flash of Elsa Datton and the other cowboys rounding up the mustang.

I believe in reincarnation. Energy is not gained nor lost, it is transformed. We, sentient beings, are made of energy. Therefore, when our bodies are no longer functioning, that energy goes somewhere else.

I want to become a sorrel mustang when my energy moves away from my body. I want to run wild and wherever I want.

The sorrel mustang is rare in the herd. I have always felt rare in the herd I am riding now on Earth.

Off till the next walk!

Who Cares?

For a long time, after my son was born, I was writing a quarterly newsletter for friends and family with the adventures of The Three Anastos.

One day, I was talking with my Aunt Petty on the phone. She asked what plans I had for the weekend, and I told her that I was going to write the newsletter. Before I could finish telling her all the other things we were planning to do, she said "Ceci, who cares about that newsletter?"

After this walk, and as I am thinking about the fate of this collection of stories, I thought whether my Aunt's opinion will hold true or not.

I hope my stories perk your curiosity to read more about some of the profound topics I have touched, and that the lighter stories bring laughter to your day.

Thank you for caring enough that you have purchased my book.

Acknowledgments

I would like to thank Siddhartha Gautama – The Buddha for the legacy he left us so we could cultivate a sound mind, and my grandma Magdalena who had the wisdom to introduce me to this philosophy of life.

Many thanks to my sisters Janice Ryan, Wendy Joplin, and Vivi Cilurzo who are constantly encouraging me to pursue my dreams, and never get tired of listening the tribulations of my busy mind.

To my childhood friends Tere Llado, Adriana Leno, Ale Basilico, Guillermo "Archi" Martinez, Dr. Marcelo Medel, Ana Carranza, Bebe and Betty Martinez, and the one and only Alfredo "Gato" Bafico Rojas. You have been unconditionally by my side when the going was getting tough, and when the fun was going full throttle.

To my publishing mentor and editor, Rick Miller, with whom I have been friends for the past 16 years. He gave me the courage to self-publish this book.

To my readers who by purchasing this book will not only financially assist me, the author, but you will make a difference for a non-profit organization named SynGAP Research Fund to whom I donate 10% of profit from the sale of this book and my paintings.

About the Author

Cecilia Anastos holds a Master's Degree in Strategic Intelligence with specialty in Middle East Issues, a Graduate Certificate in Cybercrime, a B.A. in Criminal Justice with specialty in Psychology, and a Dog Trainer degree from the Animal Behavioral College.

Ms. Anastos is also an award-winner fine artist with her art studio located in Ramona, CA; and she also trains service dogs for children with disabilities.

Fluent in five languages, she is a pioneer in the utilization of digitized open source and publicly available information to create actionable intelligence, and in the reduction of digital signatures in the cyberspace domain. She designed and taught the first cyber defense program to US Navy SEALs; as well as police departments, and private sector.

In 2016, Ms. Anastos was recognized as one of the most influential leaders in the field of cybersecurity by the San Diego Business Journal's SDBJ500; and she founded her www.meridusk9.com and art studio ceciliaanastos.com.

Ms. Anastos is an Adjunct Professor at San Diego State University where she lectures on the topics of open source information collection and analysis (OSINT), risk management when online/operational security in the cyberspace domain.

www.ingramcontent.com/pod-product-compliance
Lightning Source LLC
Chambersburg PA
CBHW071013040426
42443CB00007B/762